SEA
GLASS
SEEKER

SEA GLASS SEEKER

CINDY BILBAO

THE COUNTRYMAN PRESS

A DIVISION OF W. W. NORTON & COMPANY

Independent Publishers Since 1923

CONTENTS

INTRODUCTION

I am walking along the edge of the tide, lost in my own watery, oceanic world. I am searching the sand for glistening pieces of sea glass. Sea glass, for those who don't know, starts out as glass bottles and jars and such that end up in the ocean due to littering, shipwrecks, and various other reasons. As this glass gets tossed around and broken apart by the waves, its jagged sharp edges get worn down over time so that the pieces are rounded and smooth and the surface develops a beautiful frosted coating. All this takes approximately 40 to 50 years to develop. Rough surf dislodges this glass from the ocean's floor and brings it to the surface, where it travels the tide to settle upon whatever beach is nearby. Sea glass is relatively rare, so those lucky enough to find it often collect it and bring it home with them. Some people enjoy finding the "gems" so much they invest a lot of time and effort to locate them on the beaches.

Others tell me they would love to find sea glass during their vacations and yet they have never found any. During this lovely sunny day, while I am walking along the edge of the water, I am startled from my reverie by a gentleman who whisks past me, head down, moving very swiftly along the same section of tideline that I'm studying. He occasionally stops to pick something up and I just know he is looking for sea glass too. He moves quickly down the beach, scanning the sand. I watch him as he bends down every now and then to investigate something. He has distracted me from my search, and I fight with myself to relax and enjoy my own experience and not worry about what he is doing; yet I wonder if he has found any gems. Nevertheless, I am pretty successful because without even being aware of it, I am getting closer to the end of the beach where the gentleman was earlier, only now he is gone. It's 15 or 20 minutes after low tide—the perfect time to look for sea glass—and I am finding some beauties on the beach.

The best discovery comes when I spot a piece of orange sea glass lying in the sand about 3 feet back from the water! I am surprised that it is lying there because I know someone walked past here before I did. You

see, orange sea glass is the rarest color to find. Some people have never been able to add this color to their collections, and I was one of them until now! I shake my head in disbelief at all the colors I found that the gentleman before me missed. Why did he miss them? Well, that's what this book is all about.

There are certain things you can do to avoid being that guy on the beach who misses all the great treasures. I will give you searching tips that can increase your likelihood of coming home with a gem. The gems that can be found on beaches are not limited to glass—sometimes shards of pottery worn smooth by the sea wash up on the shore with the tide. I include these pieces of pottery when I refer to sea glass throughout this book.

CHAPTER 1

Techniques for Spotting Sea Glass

You might think that all there is to finding sea glass is looking at the sand as you walk along a beach, but that is an oversimplification. These tips will help you spot even small shards you would otherwise miss.

<< I didn't spot this pottery piece in the pebbles the first time I walked through here.

1 **Retrace your steps. Imagine that you're walking along the shoreline, making your way down the beach, taking care to look at the beach thoroughly as you go along.**

You're most likely thinking you have covered the area pretty well—and you probably have—but then, turn around and walk back through the area you've just searched. Walking in the opposite direction might seem redundant, but it is valuable to change your visual perspective as it relates to the light and the lay of the land. What you see when the light is at your back will be different from what you see when you are facing into the light because of the shadows created by rocks, shells, driftwood, seaweed, and footprints on the beach. The shadows can conceal a shard of sea glass that you could spot when you change your direction.

I always retrace my steps when I'm searching, and no matter how many times it happens, I am always shocked when I spot a shard of glass that I missed the first time around. Whether it was the glare from the sun or shadows on the beach that caused me to miss it the first time, the most important thing is that I came home that day with my treasure!

Sea glass can be partially hidden, so move along slowly and be observant. >>

<< The triangular shape of this pottery shard stands out among the rounded stones.

2 **Don't search by looking for colors alone; look for shapes as well.** Obviously, when you are beachcombing, you are looking for sea glass mostly by its color. Beautiful aqua and green colors are especially easy to see against the contrasting beige sand. But you will find more treasures by learning to train your eyes to search for shapes. Sea glass isn't always going to be a bright color that stands out. It could be a shade of white, brown, gray, or yellow that blends in with the shells, pebbles, and sand. When that's the case, the shape of

the sea glass could catch your eye instead. For instance, when there are a lot of shells or pebbles (which are mostly a rounded shape) on the beach, a rectangular or triangular shard will stand out. This is how I made one of my best finds! It was a piece of white pottery that had a faint purple design on its surface, but the beach I was searching was primarily made up of small, perfectly round, white and beige pebbles. A square shape suddenly caught my eye; the square stood out against all the round stones.

3   **Locate the high tide line.** When you first arrive at your beach, notice where the high tide mark is. This will give you a visual reference as to how far back from the water to search. The ocean reaches low tide and high tide twice in each 24-hour period. At some point each day, the tide extends onto the beach at a maximum distance for that tidal period. Along this high tide line, the ocean commonly leaves behind a trail of shells or seaweed or both, known as wrack, running perpendicular to the beach as evidence of the tide's reach. Make sure to snoop underneath this beach wrack in case it's hiding a beach treasure! Search the entire beach up to the wrack line because sea glass can be deposited anywhere in this area.

4

Move slowly. This one may seem obvious, but many people move along the beach at too brisk a pace to be able to notice everything in detail. It can be very tempting to glance at an area and determine that it is free of treasures because nothing caught your eye. I sometimes catch myself disobeying this rule and need to force myself to pause, breathe deeply, and relax into the process of beachcombing. You become more observant when you feel relaxed. The reward here isn't always the bringing away of treasures. The meditative and relaxing aspects of beachcombing are treasures too!

5

Be aware of the role that peripheral vision plays. Peripheral vision is the part of your vision that occurs beyond the center portion of your gaze. In other words, when we look at something, we see the object that is in our direct line of vision, but we also see much more than that. So in the same way that someone could be watching a child swimming in the ocean and also noticing the lifeguards

Using peripheral vision can help you spot sea glass along the edge of the water.

waving their arms some distance off to the side, we too can be looking at the sand, noticing the rocks and shells in front of us, when a different color or shape catches our attention from off to the side, just barely within our field of vision. I estimate that my peripheral vision has been responsible for as much as 40 percent of my beach finds. All it takes is an awareness of the cues that come to you peripherally and for you to be moving slowly enough to take advantage of the nuances of the beach.

Pay close attention to the shadow your body makes.
Depending upon the time of day you are on the beach, your own body can make quite a long shadow on the sand, which blocks a portion of your view. You may need to pay closer attention to the shadowed area so that you don't miss anything. Remember too that when you beachcomb with a friend, his or her shadow will also block some of your view, as yours will block theirs.

CHAPTER 2

What to Know about the Beach

1 **Early morning is a great time for beachcombing.** Normally there are far fewer people on the beach in the early morning hours—a good thing for beachcombing because there are fewer footprints in the sand to obscure your view of treasures. Sea glass can get buried in the sand during high-traffic times, making finding it even harder. I also prefer the quiet of the early-morning hours on the beach; I feel that it is the time when I can take full advantage of the emotional benefit I derive from being at the seashore. For me it's the icing on the cake! Maybe it will be for you too.

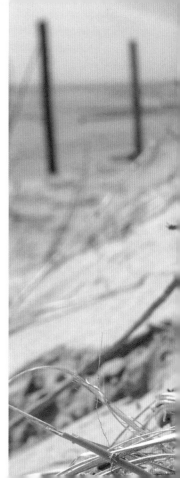

2 **Don't be discouraged if you arrive on the beach and you notice others who also appear to be looking for sea glass.** This may seem like an insignificant point to make, but some avid beachcombers (and you know who you are!) can be extremely competitive. Some beachcombers become too distracted when others are also searching. I have one particular friend who is competitive, and I am convinced that it negatively impacts her technique, causing her to feel agitated, which leads to rushing the process. As a result, often she will not find as much sea glass as I will. And those apparent competitors? The irony is that, most of the time, they're not looking for sea glass at all.

The photos above and opposite illustrate how dramatically the water level changes from high tide to low tide. In the above photo you will see two pieces of wood standing on a beach at low tide; in the middle of the photo at right you will see one of those pieces of wood barely sticking out of the water at high tide.

3 **Know the times of high tide and low tide at your beach.** In this age of technology, you can easily find out when high and low tides will be on your particular beach. For the United States, the National Oceanic and Atmospheric Administration (NOAA) has a website (www.tidesandcurrents.noaa.gov) that allows you to locate any

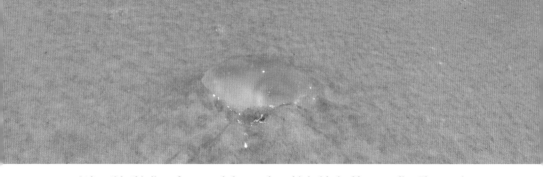

<< At low tide this line of seaweed shows where high tide had been earlier. The area in between is where you will find sea glass.

beach of interest and find out the specific times of day for high and low tide. The site offers this information for the entire year, allowing you to do this type of research long before your trip. For those of you who love having information at your fingertips, there are tide apps for your phone as well.

Knowing the time of high and low tide is one of the most important pieces of information to have when you are planning a beachcombing trip. If you arrive at the beach during high tide, you will have a very small area of sand to search. The water will be at its highest point, so you won't have much area to investigate, whereas arriving at the beach at low tide allows you the greatest area to search, giving you the potential to find more sea glass.

Know the strength of the tidal current. This is important because the strongest currents usually occur at the peak of high and low tides. The

current carries the sea glass to the beach, and so when it is at its strongest, you will be the happy recipient of its work. I have been lucky enough to be on the receiving end of numerous perfectly timed low tides, when piece after piece of beautiful, pale aqua sea glass washed up on the beach right in front of me. It's been my experience that approximately 15 to 20 minutes after low tide, during which time the tide has already reached its lowest point and is beginning its ascent back up the beach, is the best time of the whole day to find sea glass because of the strength of the current.

Knowing what phase the moon is in can benefit your search. Here again, NOAA can help you obtain that information. The NOAA website has moon phase charts for the year in advance. The tides and the moon are interconnected. The sun affects the tides as well, but the moon has greater influence, so I focus my energies on knowing the moon's phases. The moon orbits the Earth in a way that is not perfectly circular; it can be described as elliptical, so that in each orbit around the Earth it attains its closest point of approach, called the perigee, and its farthest point away from the Earth, called the apogee. The closer the moon is to the Earth, the greater the gravitational pull it exerts, and this pull directly affects ocean tides. During a full moon, high tide will be higher than it normally is and low tide will be lower than it

normally is. What this does for sea glass searchers is significant because it gives us a much greater portion of beach to look at. If you're an avid sea glass hunter, you don't want the search to end too soon! You are bound to have a more fruitful trip if you go beachcombing during a full moon.

Utilize the NOAA website to consult the tide chart for the area of your choice; it shows measurements in feet for the high and low tides each day for the current year. The most extreme tides mean the largest area of beach will be searchable. I decided to test this for myself, so I planned a beachcombing trip during a full moon. I planned to go to a beach I know well, one where I know how high an average tide usually rises, so I had a point of reference. I discovered that high and low tides are indeed greatly exaggerated during the full moon. I found that I was able to search much higher up on the beach than I usually can. I came home with a pretty cool find that day too! For those who are relatively new to beachcombing, if you try this yourselves, don't forget tip 3 in Chapter 1. When you arrive at the beach during a full moon, the first thing to do is identify the high tide line; keep in mind that it will be much farther up on the beach than you might expect.

CHAPTER 3

How to Evaluate What You've Found

The tips in this chapter won't necessarily help you find more sea glass, but they can help you bring home more treasures. These tips will teach you how to determine if a shard of sea glass is worth bringing home. They are lessons I've learned over many years, and I know my experience will benefit your beachcombing.

1 **Having a favorite color of sea glass can undermine your search.** I think every sea glass searcher secretly has a particular color that he or she covets, the color you imagine finding when you daydream (see Chapter 11 to discover your sea glass personality based on this concept). But by thinking only of the one color you are hoping to find, you are predisposing yourself to see only that color, potentially causing you to miss other pieces because they are not the color you hope to find. Try to be aware of this and train yourself to notice sea glass by its other attributes as well as by its colors.

Be aware of the frosted patina. When sea glass has a very weathered and frosted look, it's referred to as a patina. The more frosted it is, the better—this means the piece is very old and has been in the ocean at least forty or fifty years. But the very patina that makes for a highly prized find might cause you to overlook the piece altogether! The reason is because the patina has a white, frosted look **2**

This piece of white sea glass is difficult to spot because the sea foam next to it is the same color. >>

A heavily frosted chunk of sea glass can be mistaken for a rock.

that acts to camouflage the sea glass. When you find sea glass closer to the water and it's wet, the patina disappears. The water creates a sheen on the glass, making it more translucent and allowing its color to show. But when the sea glass is nestled up higher on the beach, say in the high tide line, most likely it has been there for a while and is totally dry, which makes the patina more prominent. This can make it look like a rock or pebble. This is why, when you are searching farther up on the beach, you really need to be aware that the glass will look different and its colors will not stand out as well. You need to develop sharp eyes!

3 **Don't discard a piece of sea glass based on its color.** White and brown are two of the most common colors of sea glass. Some searchers won't even bother to pick up pieces of those hues. Some beachcombers limit their collecting to only more rare colors. This can be a HUGE mistake! Pieces of the more common colors of glass often have raised lettering—commonly found on old bottles—which will give you clues about its origin or what it once contained. Beachcombers owe it to themselves to pick up brown and white shards and examine

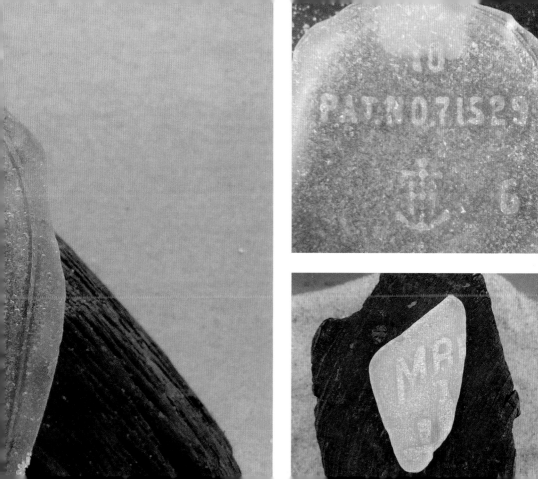

them closely. I do this all the time. If a common shard looks like it could have markings or anything unique about it, I'll put it in my basket with the rest of my finds to examine more closely later. Two of my most entertaining finds of white and brown sea glass are examples of why I do this. When I examined them later, I found that they did contain embossed words that I was able to research online, discovering whole stories behind the glass. The white piece I found contained a patent number, from which I learned the name of the man who had filed the patent back in 1926 and that it was for the design of a fancy jar. The brown piece revealed parts of words that led me to uncover a very interesting story about a company from Pennsylvania from the late 1800s that made medicines. The glass was once part of a bottle that had contained remedies or balms. I would never have discovered these cool facts if I had overlooked those pieces of sea glass based on the fact that they were just common white or brown glass. These old pieces of sea glass sometimes have whole histories behind them, and they can present a fun mystery to unravel!

4 **Hold dark pieces up to the sun to verify their color.** Here is another tip for people who tend to overlook the basic, common brown shard of sea glass: Darker brown pieces of sea glass might actually be red, and red sea glass is one of the rarest colors out there. According to Richard LaMotte in his book, *Pure Sea Glass: Discovering Nature's Vanishing Gems*, the chance of finding red

Both of these pieces appear to be brown. However, one of them is really an extremely rare red color. The difference becomes obvious when you allow the light to pass through the glass.

sea glass is 1 in 5,000. He categorizes red as being extremely rare. I don't know about you, but I would hate to miss this opportunity because I failed to notice that a piece of glass was something more interesting than a common brown piece. This is exactly what almost happened to me one day. There was a smallish, rectangular shard of glass lying in the sand that appeared to be dark brown. I actually did pass it by, because there were quite a few brown pieces on the beach that day. But after walking a few steps away from it, I thought that I should at least investigate it fully before I wrote it off. (See previous tip.) So I went back and picked it up— but it wasn't until I held it up to the sky so the light could pass through it that I realized I had a beautiful, rare piece of red glass! I almost passed out! To imagine that I'd passed it by the first time—oh, man! I can relate to you a similar story about almost passing up a rare, deep purple insulator from an old light bulb because it looked like a black rock in the sand, as there were several shells and dark colored rocks on this beach. I did pick it up—I learned my lesson well—and held it up to the sky, and just around the outside, where the glass was thinner, I could see that the color was actually a deep purple! This became one of my unique finds!

5 **If you're unsure whether what you've found is sea glass, hold it up to the sky.** Just as with the light bulb insulator, the light can reveal a true find. While this is not a fail-safe test because some treasures will be pottery or china, and therefore not transparent, it can help you determine if your find is not glass but a rock or shell fragment. Don't discard it until you are sure. Glass will let light through, especially if you wet it before you hold it up to the light.

Examine your finds more carefully at home. Take your time, really look at and feel your treasure so you can determine whether you have something really unique that can take center stage in your **6**

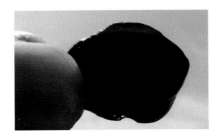

collection. Very old black glass bottles from the early 1800s have a thick base and, because the glass is black, it isn't really transparent. I found a perfectly round, well-frosted piece of black sea

Sunlight reveals the faint purple color around the edges of this very old light bulb insulator.

Very old and extremely rare black glass.

glass that at first I really thought was a flat black pebble that would be a nice size to paint a small picture on, so I took it home. It didn't pass my light test, so I really thought it was a rock. It wasn't until I got it home and really took the time to examine it that I realized I could feel a texture on the surface, so I took a closer look. I was able to just barely make out a word that was nearly worn off! It was then that I learned that I had found the bottom of a very, very old bottle.

Lay your treasures out on something white. Against a white backdrop, shards you thought were also white often prove to be pale pink, yellow, or another color. Upon arriving home from one of my beachcombing trips several years ago, I arranged my glass on a white towel outside. Then one of my kids called me. When I returned to my finds, I was amazed to notice that one of the pieces I thought was white when it was still damp had completely dried and was actually a rare light pink color. Since that day, I've made it a habit to lay out my finds on a white surface after every trip. I've since discovered that there are quite a few pieces in my collection that are not white but rather a light shade of purple, yellow, gray, or aqua.

7

<< Subtle hues show up better against a white background.

CHAPTER 4

Know the Weather

Weather is one of those things we can easily take for granted. These tips tell you why serious beachcombers know never to do that.

<< Stronger waves help to transport sea glass to shore.

1 **Wind can create larger waves.** Anybody who loves the beach knows the effects of wind on water. The wind blowing into shore can affect the waves, increasing their size and strength. These stronger waves have greater potential to carry shells, sea glass, and debris from the ocean to the shore. If you pay attention to the weather forecast for your particular beach and to note to the wind speed and direction (easterly is what you want), you could have an advantage. Look for a correlation between an increase in easterly winds at the time of day that low tide is transitioning back to high tide (see Chapter 2, tip 3), and you could have the makings of a good beachcombing excursion.

2 **Go beachcombing after storms.** If you are able to plan a beach excursion after a storm, you may be rewarded for your efforts by finding some nice treasures left behind by the wind and waves. The effects of the stronger currents, wave action, and erosion can dislodge and uncover long-buried treasures and bring them to the beach.

Active coastal storm seasons can provide good beachcombing for years to come. Sometimes a single storm will not be enough to uncover deeply buried glass, but the powerful effects of wind and surf from numerous storms work to dislodge sea glass that could have been buried for decades. For example, a hurricane followed by a strong winter storm could wash many treasures to the shorelines and beaches so you will have the chance to find them. Chapter 10 has additional information on storms. **3**

4 **Fall and spring are the best seasons for beachcombing.**
If you're excited to get out on a beach and start finding sea glass, you may be disappointed when I tell you that summer is the worst season to find these treasures. Winter is actually preferable to summer when it comes to beachcombing for sea glass. But since most of us prefer to vacation at the seashore during the summer, do look for it then, just be aware of the obstacles and how to work around them.

In summer a few factors make sea glass more difficult to find, but it's not impossible. First, there are so many people at the beach and so many footsteps helping to bury the glass. Also, during summer months many public beaches are swept at night so the sand will be soft and free of debris for the public to enjoy the next morning. Any sea glass that would have been washed ashore in the evening hours will be buried. In the springtime, before the official beach season gets under way and before all the crowds arrive, you will find the beach in its more natural state, making it a great time to visit. Fall is my favorite time to search for sea glass, however. The beaches get quieter after the season ends and the crowds leave, but the weather is still mild. But in my experience, later in the autumn season and early in the winter months is the best time to search for sea glass. The hurricane season begins in late summer and continues into November. During this time, the strong surf created by the stormy weather rips across the ocean floor, helping to dislodge all sorts of treasures that are swept up onto the beach. We know that good-quality sea glass is at least forty or fifty years old, and it has most likely been buried for much of that time. The strong current that is the result of high wind and wave action during hurricane season helps to uncover all sorts of goodies.

5

Overcast days are the best days to look for sea glass.
Most beachgoers choose the sunniest days to be at the seashore, but sea glass enthusiasts should choose to go on cloudy days. On bright, sunny days there will be lots of glare on the water and the sand, making it very difficult to see anything. Bright sun also creates deep shadows that can hide sea glass. Clouds on an overcast day help diffuse the light, making it easier to see what you're looking for.

Clouds help to diffuse sunlight, making cloudy days better than sunny days for searching the beach. >>

CHAPTER 5

Your Attire: Comfort Is Key

Tips for how to dress for beachcombing might sound superfluous, but they are anything but! Whether it is sunny or stormy out, hot or cold, what you wear to the beach will help or hinder your searching, so be prepared.

1 **Beachcombers with longer hair should ALWAYS bring something to tie it back with.** Bring along a hat, headband, hair elastic, bandanna—whatever works for you—every time you go beachcombing, even if there's no breeze. This is one of the most important tips in this book, and I discovered it the hard way! Just imagine it: You're looking forward to a fabulous day of treasure hunting, but the breeze picks up and your hair is suddenly flying across your face, blowing in your eyes and mouth, tickling your cheeks and nose. You can't see to walk down the beach, let alone to spot shards of sea glass. Holding it out of the way will make you crazy, especially when you want to pick up something. Half the enjoyment of beachcombing is the relaxation you feel while you're doing it, and flying, wild hair will quickly destroy that!

Consider not wearing sunglasses. Tinted sunglasses change the color of everything you see. They will alter the colors of sea glass on the sand, and that can cause you to miss it. A blue piece of sea glass, for instance, could look gray through sunglasses; you may take it for a shell or driftwood and pass it by. I suggest wearing a **2**

baseball cap instead—that's what I do. Of course, some people must shield their eyes with sunglasses for health reasons, but if you don't have to wear them, try beachcombing without them.

3 **Know your weather conditions.**
As I previously mentioned, the off-seasons at the beach are best for sea glass hunting. But that means that you will not always encounter great weather. Being comfortable will help you be more successful, so it is very important to know what the weather will be like so you can dress accordingly and feel comfortable. Most of the time, I find I need a hat and scarf, but I forgo the gloves, opting instead to stick my hands in my warm coat pockets (better make sure your coat has pockets!).

4 **Wear waterproof shoes.** Unlike summertime beach visits, when you want to be barefoot, during the fall, winter, and even spring months, the sand is cold—very cold—and the water is even colder. I have had great excursions made very uncomfortable when my feet got wet from a surprise wave I couldn't get out of the way of in time. Once I'd bought warm, waterproof boots that go up to my knees, I was all set! No amount of errant surf ruined my day ever again.

Consider an anorak-style jacket. With a zippered pocket in the front to hold your treasures, an anorak is a great option for the person who doesn't like to carry anything while beachcombing. I personally prefer to carry a big plastic bag with a zip top, with a smaller, sandwich-sized plastic bag inside it. The reason for the two sizes is that anything larger and heavier can go in the large bag, but it's a good idea to separate the smaller or more fragile pieces of glass. The weight of the larger items can actually break the smaller and more **5**

<< Rubber boots help keep feet dry when you're searching close to the water in the colder months.

fragile pieces, so put them in the smaller bag and carry it. Either way, you have to find what works best for you. First decide if you want to carry something around with you or if you prefer to be empty-handed, and then go from there.

Consider investing in good rain gear. I mean the works—a nice GORE-TEX jacket and pants. When you're looking for sea glass on the beach, carrying an umbrella just isn't practical. You might not be obsessed enough to go out there in the pouring rain, but my fellow hard-core searchers know that I'm not exaggerating when I say I go out rain or shine. Only lightning will keep me away from the beach, so good rain gear is very important.

CHAPTER 6

Know the Location

The best place to search for sea glass is in an area
that has reasons why old broken glass would be resting
in sand at the bottom of the ocean.

Spend some time researching various regions of the coast you'd like to
visit. Determine if an area would be a good place to find sea glass. There
are five factors to pay attention to in order to determine areas where old
glass might be buried. Along coastlines around the world, there are many,
many places like this.

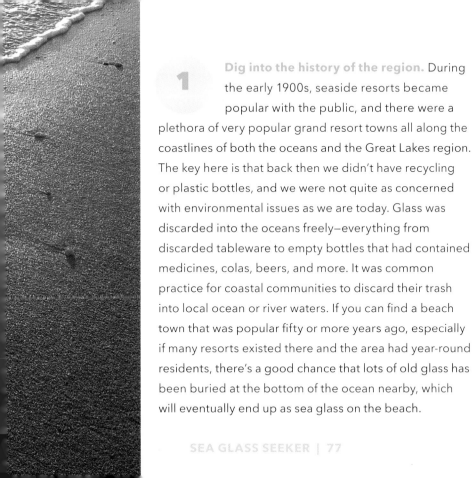

1 **Dig into the history of the region.** During the early 1900s, seaside resorts became popular with the public, and there were a plethora of very popular grand resort towns all along the coastlines of both the oceans and the Great Lakes region. The key here is that back then we didn't have recycling or plastic bottles, and we were not quite as concerned with environmental issues as we are today. Glass was discarded into the oceans freely—everything from discarded tableware to empty bottles that had contained medicines, colas, beers, and more. It was common practice for coastal communities to discard their trash into local ocean or river waters. If you can find a beach town that was popular fifty or more years ago, especially if many resorts existed there and the area had year-round residents, there's a good chance that lots of old glass has been buried at the bottom of the ocean nearby, which will eventually end up as sea glass on the beach.

2 **Locate beaches near areas where there used to be lots of manufacturing.** Chances are, these old factories discarded glass regularly into the ocean or local river systems, as was the common practice. Back in the 1800s manufacturing areas tended to be located near waterways because water was a needed resource for both manufacturing and shipping.

Find beaches that are close to old shipping ports. If a beach is close to a shipping route, there's a strong possibility that, long ago, glass and pottery were thrown overboard. In times past, it was common for ships to carry heavy pottery as ballast, which sometimes got discarded into the water when it was no longer needed. Also, passengers on ships often discarded refuse into the waterways, because at that time it was not known to be environmentally harmful. **3**

 Look for local shipwrecks. If you can find a beach near old shipping routes, do some research to learn whether that area had any shipwrecks. Shipwrecks are plentiful up and down

the Atlantic coast, for example, and many a ship's cargo has been lost to the sea. Sea glass in the form of old pottery, old glass fragments, and even gold and silver coins from these wrecks, swept up onto the beaches a hundred years later, is, in my opinion, the ultimate find. To me, the notion of finding such beach treasure is indeed the most romantic.

Learn whether there are any rivers that empty into the ocean nearby. These rivers often bring huge amounts of old glass to the ocean, especially if they run near cities where factories and manufacturing plants once discarded their trash.

5

Evaluating Locations Using These Five Factors

There are certain parts of coastline that have far better potential for sea glass than others. By using the above criteria you can discover them on your own. The intent of this section is to show you how to apply the investigative work to the area of coastline that you are considering visiting. In the following examples, I have used these criteria to analyze parts of the New England and Mid-Atlantic coastlines, but they can be applied to any coastal regions in the world.

Coastal Maine has a rich history of tourism around the turn of the twentieth century. In the town of Bar Harbor, in northern Maine, a hotel-building boom resulted in many lavish accommodations around that time. The rich and famous vacationed and built majestic estates in this area. In the late 1880s, tourism was the major industry in Bar Harbor. Large inns such as the Rodick House contained some 400 guest rooms, which attracted many tourists. Because of this history, the beaches of Bar Harbor and surrounding areas such as the Cranberry Isles and Mount Desert Island would be very good places to search for sea glass that originally might have been decorative dishware, pottery, and glassware owned by the region's wealthy visitors or used to serve guests in the area's hotels.

After exploring the Bar Harbor area, drive south along Route 1 to discover the areas around Camden and Rockland. Here the Penobscot River empties into Penobscot Bay. Wherever a larger river system empties into local bays or oceans is a great place to beachcomb. In this area, however, the beachcombing could be particularly good because there was heavy commerce in Bangor in the 1850s. At that time, Bangor was

one of the busiest ports on the East Coast, and it was common to dump garbage in the water. Bits of broken bottles and glassware discarded into the river would eventually reach the bay and ocean. Another factor making this area noteworthy is that Rockland's harbor saw a lot of industrial activity. During the nineteenth century more than 10,000 ships came and went out of the bay annually. With that amount of shipping traffic, glass should definitely be found in the waters offshore. Based on these factors, I would recommend searching the beaches along the coast from Belfast to Camden, including Deer Isle in Penobscot Bay.

Continue south to the Portland area. It is here that the Kennebec River runs into Casco Bay, so the beaches in this region of Cape Elizabeth, Maine, are excellent areas to find sea glass. Portland developed as a commercial port as early as the 1790s, and it is considered Maine's economic capital because it is the largest port in the state. There are also many shipwrecks in the waters surrounding Portland, another source of sea glass.

A little south of Portland, where the Saco River empties into Saco Bay, is another area long favored by tourists, Old Orchard Beach. It has been a vacation destination since the 1800s. Because of the river, the history of tourism, and this area's proximity to Portland's shipping lanes, I recommend following Route 1 south throughout the area, including Kennebunkport and Ogunquit and even farther south to York, to find beaches that should provide a wealth of sea glass.

MASSACHUSETTS

Gloucester, located on Cape Ann, and its surrounding beaches should provide plenty of sea treasures. One of the reasons is that many generations of people visited and lived here. Gloucester was the second permanent settlement after the Pilgrims landed at Plymouth in 1620; it was established as a fishing harbor as early as the 1700s. Gloucester quickly became one of the largest fishing ports in the world, and it still generates a great deal of sailing traffic. This fact, plus the more than 300 shipwrecks that have occurred in the waters offshore, contribute to the supply of sea glass here. Based on all these factors I would recommend a drive along Route 127, which follows the perimeter of Cape Ann and continues south toward Manchester, Massachusetts. Any beaches you discover along the way would be worth your time to visit.

The coastal city of Boston undoubtedly provides an excellent source for sea glass along the many miles of beaches north and south of the city. This glass most likely comes here via the Charles River, which travels through twenty-three cities before it empties into the Atlantic Ocean. By the nineteenth century, this river was one of the most industrialized areas in the US. Boston also housed approximately a dozen businesses that manufactured pottery, porcelain, or glass in the 1800s—another source of sea treasures.

Plymouth, Massachusetts, is "America's Hometown," the site of the first colony in America. Plymouth Harbor supported fishing and shipping in the 1800s. Beaches in this area should therefore be reliable places to find sea glass.

Cape Cod is also among the Massachusetts areas whose principal industries since the 1800s have been fishing, shipping, and tourism. Another thing that makes this area so interesting a place to search for sea glass is the more than 1,000 shipwrecks in the waters that surround it. These wrecks are the reason many refer to this area as the ocean's graveyard. At least some of the items in the cargos of those ships would eventually become today's sea glass treasures. Two of the more famous shipwrecks I find to be particularly intriguing from a beachcombing perspective are the *Whydah* and the *John S. Dwight*. In 1717, the *Whydah*, a pirate ship, went down off the coast of Cape Cod at Wellfleet. Did the ship indeed carry a treasure trove of gold and silver as is commonly thought? Might someone find some of the coins it was carrying on a beach one day? You never know! The *John S. Dwight* went down in 1923. This vessel was used for rum-running and was carrying a cargo of bootleg ale in glass bottles, and, as we know, old bottles often become sea glass treasures. It is also pertinent to note that a glass manufacturer was operating in Sandwich, Massachusetts, in the 1800s. Wherever there are old coastal glassworks, it is possible to find sea glass on the surrounding beaches because it was common for trash to be dumped into waterways. I believe that beachcombers could find significant amounts of sea glass on any of the Cape Cod beaches, but I recommend searching in the Provincetown area that sits at the very end of the Cape.

Newport was one of the leading ports in the mid-1700s, and when you take into account that nearby Providence was one of the first US cities to become industrialized, you can understand why Rhode Island had some of the largest manufacturing plants in the region by the early twentieth century. Anytime this type of early growth takes place in a coastal city, you can be sure that there is great potential for finding old sea glass on nearby beaches.

Another contributing factor is that there was a huge real estate boom during the 1850s that resulted in the construction of many opulent summer homes. In fact, Newport became known for its splendor and for attracting the wealthy. For this reason, I would expect that some of the sea glass found here probably originated from expensive and decorative dinnerware and glassware, likely beautiful and varied in color. It is also interesting to note that the rum industry was strong in Rhode Island in the mid-1760s. At that time there were approximately twenty-two distilleries operating in Newport—another great source of sea glass!

By the late 1800s New Jersey had become the center of US glass manufacturing because it contained an abundance of the silica sand, wood, and water needed for the process. In fact, the Whitall Tatum Company, located in Millville, was one of the first glass factories in America; it operated from 1806 until 1938.

The Trenton area, because of its proximity to the shores of the Delaware River, was home to approximately forty-five different glass manufacturers from the late 1800s until the early 1900s. The Delaware River also plays a very important role because it empties into the Delaware Bay. Cape May sits at the very tip of the state and has beaches along both the Delaware Bay and the Atlantic Ocean. The beaches of New Jersey benefit from the existence of more than 2,000 shipwrecks off the coast and a rich, long history of tourism in the area. Cape May is my favorite place to hunt for sea glass when I am unable to go too far from home, but I also recommend any of the state's beautiful beaches.

DELAWARE

Similar to the other East Coast locations discussed, Delaware's proximity to a major river system marks it as a great spot for sea glass hunting. The Delaware River carries sea glass to this area, just as it does in New Jersey. Delaware's waters also have their share of shipwrecks.

OTHER LOCATIONS

I'll stop here, but you don't have to—in fact, please don't! There are so many wonderful places in the world to have your own adventures. For instance, check out these beaches that are named for the glass that's been found on them:

- **Sea Glass Beach**, Bermuda
- **Glass Beach**, Puerto Rico
- **Broken Glass Beach**, Key West, Florida
- **Glass Beach**, Port Townsend, Washington
- **Glass Beach**, Fort Bragg, California
- **Glass Beach**, Kauai, Hawaii
- **Bottle Beach**, Thailand

CHAPTER 7

Materials Your Treasures Might Be Made Of

Much of the older sea glass found on beaches in areas that saw heavy tourism in the 1800s could be anything from various types of decorative glass to several kinds of pottery. It is interesting to note the origins of some of the pieces we find along the beach. Here is a rundown of what was popular back in that time period.

Above: Vaseline glass Right: Milk glass

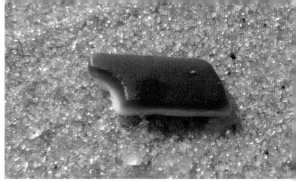

Left: Semi-porcelain pottery shard from the 19th century.
Right: Flashed glass, made by layering colored glass and white glass.

Carnival glass is pressed glass that has an iridescent finish that gives
it a metallic surface luster. Carnival glass was produced from 1905
through the early 1930s.

English ironstone china is solid white tableware that was made from
1813 through 1860. It was imported to the US beginning in the 1840s
and was manufactured in the US in the 1850s.

Malachite glass is another pressed glass with colored swirls made to
look like marble. Malachite glass was produced in green, purple, or
brown in the late nineteenth and early twentieth centuries.

Milk glass is an opaque pressed glass that is often white, blue, green, or pink. It was made from 1840 through 1960.

Neodymium glass is also known as Alexandrite glass. This fancy glass changes color under natural and artificial light. Neodymium glass was made from about 1930 through 1950.

Pearline glass is pressed glass, usually a yellow or blue color, with an opalescent rim. Pearline glass was manufactured from 1889 through 1914.

Vaseline glass is a pale yellowish-green color similar to the color of petroleum jelly. The glass was made with uranium oxide, which causes the glass to glow a bright green under ultraviolet light. Vaseline glass was produced from 1880 through 1920.

Wedgwood pottery started production in 1765 and continues today. Three types of Wedgwood were especially popular in the eighteenth and nineteenth centuries:

- Queensware is cream-colored earthenware.
- Black Basalt is black porcelain stoneware.
- Jasperware is blue and white.

A rare frosted marble that could have been a child's toy or from a Codd-neck bottle for carbonated beverages, produced from the late 1800s to the early 1900s, which featured a marble in the neck of the bottle.

Some of the sea glass we find on beaches today comes from shipwrecks or working ships entering and leaving the many ports along the coast. Here is a brief rundown of what their cargo might have contained as it relates to sea glass treasures:

- Glass oil lamps
- Porcelain figures
- Pressed glass and porcelain tableware and decorative items
- Gold and silver coins
- Elegant glassware
- Ceramic dish sets, pitchers, and crocks
- Marbles

Color and Patina

One of the more obvious features of sea glass is its frosted appearance. Called its patina, it is just one of the beautiful effects that salty ocean water has on glass.

The basic ingredients of glass are soda, sand, and lime. These natural elements are eventually break down and disintegrate when glass is submerged in ocean water for a very long time. As the glass sits in the ocean it goes through a process called hydration, in which the lime and soda in the glass are leached out by years of contact with seawater. The lime and soda join with other elements to form crystallization on the glass's surface, creating the frosted appearance of the sea glass. This patina is the cause of the beautiful glow that sea glass has when the light hits it just right, bringing out beautiful colors.

When artisans create new glass vessels, they add various chemical oxides to the basic mix of soda, lime, and sand to obtain color. Here is a brief overview of how color was originally attained in your sea glass treasures:

- Blue comes from cobalt oxide or copper.
- Red comes from gold oxide (red glass was not often produced in the 1800s).
- Green is the result of added chromium or copper.
- Purple is the result of added magnesium oxide. (An interesting note is that this color deepens the longer it is exposed to the ultraviolet light of the sun.)
- Yellow comes from uranium.
- Brown is the result of added ceric oxide.
- Black comes from iridium oxide.

- Amber is derived from added nickel, sulfur, or carbon.
- Aqua is the natural color of glass when nothing is added. It comes from impurities in iron, which is found naturally in the sand that is a major component of glass.
- Clear glass is obtained by adding either manganese dioxide or selenium dioxide.

Erosion also helps shards lose their sharp edges. The shards are tumbled and rolled around on the ocean floor, working down any sharp points over time.

CHAPTER 9

Storms Affecting Beachcombing

Sometimes the best beachcombing experiences can occur after stormy weather, when it's almost guaranteed that you will find some interesting things on the beach. For an improved opportunity at finding sea glass, try to plan a beach visit after a storm or a period of high coastal winds.

Every year storms and hurricanes batter our coastlines, shifting great amounts of sand from our beaches. Sometimes this weather uncovers far more than simple sea glass. Over the past several years, numerous storms have revealed remnants of shipwrecked vessels right on the beaches in different areas of the US. Many of these sailing vessels are very old and difficult to positively identify, but they can fuel the imagination of many a beachcomber hoping to uncover a fragment of a very old bottle or glass that might have been part of the cargo of the sunken ship.

Superstorm Sandy helped to reveal the skeleton of a shipwreck from the 1920s on Fire Island Beach on Long Island, New York.

An early March storm in 2013 battered the shoreline in Maine, revealing a vessel from the early 1800s.

Several hurricanes over the past 15 years helped to uncover a large wooden ship on a private island in Alabama, and El Niño-related storms on the Pacific Coast during 2015 revealed the remains of a 1930s ship on a beach in Southern California.

Try to plan a beachcombing trip after a storm. >>

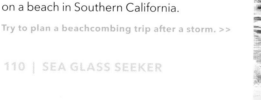

An early November 2014 storm unearthed a shipwrecked vessel on Chappaquiddick, Martha's Vineyard, that possibly dates back to the 1800s.

This same early November storm uncovered a section of old railroad tracks originally built back in 1905 on the beach in Cape May, New Jersey. Railroad tracks are an unusual sight to see on a beach, alongside the crashing waves. They had been part of a sand excavation business there in the early 1900s and had been buried under the sand for about 80 years until the storm on November 1-3, 2014, battered the coastline with 50 mph winds and coastal flooding. I visited the area a few weeks later, eager for some beachcombing time. The tracks were still visible and quite a sight to see, eerily disappearing into the sand seemingly without end. The receding tide had formed a gully around the exposed tracks so that a few inches of still water engulfed them, leaving only the highest parts of the tracks dry. Through the few inches of water I could see sand, pebbles, and rusted metal. The sea glass-searching instinct ever present in me spotted an odd shape partially buried in the sand surrounding the tracks under the water. It didn't look like it was part of the track system, and it didn't

I pulled this Hemingray insulator out of the water and sand right beside this track. >>

seem like it was a shell, but I couldn't see it well enough to know what it was and I had to put my hand into the water to pull it out. Nervously (the water was very cold and I didn't know what I was about to touch), I reached in and pulled the object out, fully expecting it to be a rock—which it definitely was not! What I pulled out of the water was part of an old insulator with a pretty scalloped edge in a beautiful turquoise color. It was such an exciting discovery, and I began to contemplate how it might have gotten there to begin with. I imagined that it had gotten snagged by the tracks on the beach many, many years ago—probably during the 1930s, when the tracks had last been uncovered by the sand. Most likely it became lodged there and went on to be buried under layers of sand and water for all those years until the storm and the tides uncovered it enough for me to spy. Researching it later, I discovered that it was a "Hemingray No. 52" telegraph insulator produced from the 1890s through the 1910s.

The weather patterns of 2014 and 2015 stand in stark contrast with each other. The weather plays such an important role for beachcombers,

<< This section of old railway tracks became exposed on a beach in Cape May after an early November storm swept the coast in 2014.

affecting both what we may uncover as storms roll by and our very ability to search the beach. During the brutal winter of 2014, many areas in New England were covered in so much snowfall that getting to the beach was impossible. Winter Storm Hercules dumped more than a foot of snow on Massachusetts, Vermont, New Hampshire, and New York, and then Winter Storm Pax crippled many Mid-Atlantic states. It was a rough winter with places like Boston experiencing six major snowstorms. I remember fellow beachcombers who love searching in the winter months lamenting about their inability to get to the beach.

The following December (2015) was just the opposite. I was sitting on a New Jersey beach on December 13 comfortably wearing shorts. It was so warm that it could easily have been a beautiful day in June. I was able to enjoy a wonderful weekend of beach weather in comfortable temperatures for beachcombing in December!

Each season, hurricanes and winter storms along the coast change the profile of the beach. If you pay attention to what areas were affected by weather, you can plan your adventures with maximum effect and, with some good luck, you will come home with some wonderful treasures!

CHAPTER 10

Your Journal

Whenever you set out searching for treasures, there are limitless possibilities before you: where and when to go, techniques to employ, weather reports to be aware of, and moon phases to look up.

If you choose to, you can gather a lot of useful information for your trip. In this chapter, I want to give you the space to record and organize it all. It can also serve as a record that you could refer back to if you want to compare data from each trip. Sometimes it's also interesting to look back in your records to see the beach, the date, and the weather conditions when you found a particularly special piece of sea glass.

Trip Date, Location, and Time	Weather Report	Time of High Tide	Time of Low Tide	Moon Phase	Sea Glass Found	Colors

CHAPTER 11

What Is Your Sea Glass Personality?

In that moment when you first arrive at the beach, as you take that first deep breath of salty ocean air and first step onto the sand to search for sea glass, your mind's eye knows what color sea glass you really want to find.

As you gaze across the sand, there is a particular color that you most want to see lying there. It is not the color you want to find that day because you want to complete your collection and you still need to find a red piece, or you're creating a piece of jewelry with your sea glass and you need to find

a green piece. What I'm talking about is that pigment that most pleases you when you discover it. It's the color that takes your breath away when you spot it, whether white, lime or clover green, chartreuse, cobalt blue, purple, yellow, aqua, sea foam green, teal, harbor blue, red, pink, orange, or brown. That hue is the essence of your sea glass personality. What does that color reveal about you? What characteristics are you likely to possess given your preference for that color? Take a moment to imagine you are about to embark on a sea glass-finding mission, and without giving it a lot of thought, zero in on the color you favor over all the others. Read on to see what your choice says about you.

White: If white is the color you most enjoy finding, it means that you desire simplicity in your life. Maybe your life is complex or stressful, and you'd like it to be less so. Perhaps life is already the way you like it, but something threatens the calm you've created. You come to the seashore as often as you can because it is there that you feel happiest. People who are drawn to white sea glass might feel the need to make time to get to the beach often in order to relax, restore, and keep their emotions on an even keel.

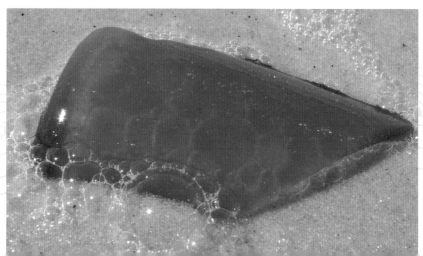

Lime Green: You are likely very gregarious and outgoing. You enjoy having fun and being active outdoors. You probably are not very fashion conscious and hate to shop. You are very loyal and will go out of your way to help your friends. Your love of the beach comes from your sense of adventure, and you tend to travel a lot. Lime green sea glass fans feel a need to visit many different beaches, so you might not have a favorite.

Clover Green: Outdoorsy and active, you stay indoors as little as possible. You enjoy participating in solitary activities more than in team sports. You have a very calm nature, and people enjoy being in your company. You strive to find the perfect mix of social interaction and quiet time alone, requiring both in your life. Clover green sea glass people visit the beach often, but usually it is with someone different each time.

Chartreuse (Yellow-Green): You are very adventurous and assertive. You enjoy having a great deal of power in your life, especially positions of leadership. People tend to look up to you. You can be bold and a

little outspoken at times. Chartreuse sea glass people are not content to beachcomb in sleepy, quiet areas; places like Atlantic City suit them better.

Cobalt Blue: With a tendency toward moodiness, you have to be careful not to brood. You are very emotional and capable of deep feelings, so you form many rewarding relationships. You are sensitive and enjoy helping others. You might not excel at staying organized, and your home environment isn't always the neatest, but your strong, caring personality draws people in. Those who favor cobalt sea glass enjoy the beach all year long, not only in the summer.

Purple: You have a strong desire to be unique and you don't mind calling attention to yourself. You tend to be a very loyal friend, and you are most likely an animal lover. Characterized by a very positive attitude, you also display very good taste and like to surround yourself with beautiful and sometimes expensive things. Purple sea glass people go out of their way to find the best beaches in extremely beautiful places.

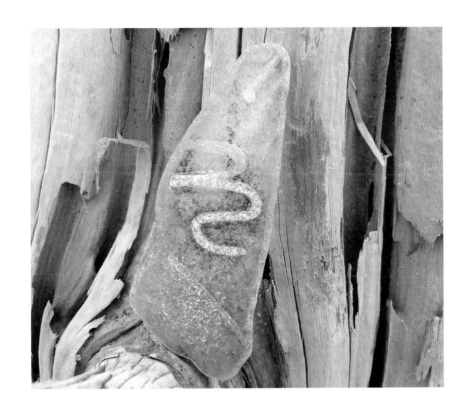

Yellow: Very imaginative with an upbeat personality, you have a great sense of humor and are generally a happy soul. You are likely to have more than one pet. Your home is decorated with bold, happy colors. You also enjoy cooking for friends—a yellow sea glass person is the one who loves to pack the picnic basket, gather a group of friends, and head to the beach for the day.

Aqua: Artistic and imaginative, you tend to be positive, but you often live in your own little world, trying to distance yourself from the harsh realities of life. You appreciate and surround yourself with the beauty of nature and fully immerse yourself in the meditative feeling of the seashore. Aqua sea glass people truly need to be near the water, and finding this color sea glass is for them like taking home a reminder of the sea itself.

Sea Foam Green: You are mild mannered and outwardly mellow. However, that façade hides much inner turmoil. You tend to be a nervous person, and sometimes you have difficulty concentrating. You love to read and can be quite imaginative, and you are also a homebody, often quite content to be in your own company. In fact, for you, Sea Foam Green, trips to the beach might be the only time you really enjoy being far away from home.

Teal: You are someone who sets high standards—for yourself and others. You have a strong desire to succeed, and therefore you can be quite competitive and impatient at times. You are athletic and you love the water, often combining the two for entertainment. You find traveling very exciting and rewarding, so you're often on the move. If teal sea glass is your favorite, you probably look to a beach vacation for your next adventure.

Harbor Blue: You are compassionate, caring, and sensitive. Friends often come to you with their problems, and you have a difficult time saying "no" to anyone in need. Harbor Blues are hard workers, sometimes needing to be convinced to take a vacation, but when they do get away the seashore is always their first choice.

Red: You are an extrovert, at your best when you're busy. But make sure to throw a ton of fun into the mix because you can never have too much

of a good time. Always ready for entertainment, your motto is "Work hard and play harder." You love to travel, and often do. Red sea glass fans will travel the world, enjoying many different beaches.

Pink: You have a strong desire to feel loved unconditionally, and you need to feel accepted. You feel most comfortable when you are part of the crowd. However, you are also an extremely fun person to be around, and you have a great personality. A very hard worker, you might get impatient with those who don't share this trait with you. Pink sea glass people love to be at the beach with a group of family or friends.

Orange: You can be a little shy in situations that are new to you, but you work very hard to hide it. When you are in your comfort zone, watch out! This is where your personality shines. You enjoy trying new things, and you tend to get bored easily. You will move from one project to the next without fully completing the first one. Your mind races and you might have difficulty sleeping at night. Orange sea glass people need the quiet and calm they find at the seashore.

Brown: You are content and comfortable with who you are, and you have a solid set of values that you live your life by. You are optimistic and display strong coping skills when life throws you a curveball. Others describe you as being down-to-earth and very likable. Brown sea glass people have a favorite beach they will return to again and again.

AUTHOR'S NOTE

I have been photographing images in nature for as long as I can remember. Over the years, coastal venues have become my favorite place to take pictures and sea glass is a natural extension of that subject matter. Photographing sea glass began as a way for me to preserve that special moment of discovery which is such a magical sliver of time.

My sea glass photographing journey first began during one particular beachcombing occasion. The antithetical appearance of a large, glowing aqua color gleaming against the quiet stillness and stark emptiness of the beach with no footprints, shells, or other debris in the sand startled me. The mood this created was something I wanted to capture and remember so I snapped a few quick pictures. After that I was hooked. The ever-shifting moods of the seashore complement the mystery and sense of adventure surrounding sea glass and that is what I strive to depict in my photos.

I love capturing images of sea glass in its natural found location before I pick it up, but sometimes that is not possible—either because I don't want to risk losing the piece to the incoming waves or the natural light is not good. Some of the shots I take are carefully set up in order to get the best use of the light or scenery of the area. Some of my favorite shots are ones that depict an entire scene and the sea glass is the secondary subject because it tells a whole story or sets a mood.

Because of the sheer beauty of the natural surroundings where sea glass is found, and the unique beauty of sea glass itself, it is a subject that I will always enjoy photographing, and through these pages I hope you will enjoy this journey with me.

—Cindy Bilbao

Please visit my website, where beachcombers and beach lovers can find unique gifts that I personally have had a hand in developing: www.SeaGlassSearchersClub.com

You can also follow Sea Glass Searchers Club on Facebook and Instagram (@seaglasssearchersclub).

ACKNOWLEDGMENTS

Thanks, Mom, for being my beachcombing partner for all these years. We sure have some funny stories to tell of our many crazy experiences! That's what it's all about, creating fond memories.

And a word of thanks to my friend Victoria Tesoniero for her proofreading skills that helped me get my words and thoughts together for this book.

You never know what your sea glass searching experience will be like from one day to the next, but if the tide is right and you are in the right place at the right time, you will find your treasure!

For information about permission to reproduce selections from this book, write to Permissions, The Countryman Press, 500 Fifth Avenue, New York, NY 10110

For information about special discounts for bulk purchases, please contact W. W. Norton Special Sales at specialsales@wwnorton.com or 800-233-4830

Manufacturing through Imago
Book design by Weller Smith Design
Production manager: Devon Zahn

Library of Congress Cataloging-in-Publication Data
Names: Bilbao, Cindy, author.
Title: Sea glass seeker / Cindy Bilbao.
Other titles: Official sea glass searcher's guide
Description: New York, NY : The Countryman Press, a division of W. W. Norton & Company, [2017] | "This book was published in a slightly different form as The Official Sea Glass Searcher's Guide by Countryman Press in 2014."
Identifiers: LCCN 2016059478 | ISBN 9781682681169 (pbk.)
Subjects: LCSH: Sea glass—Collectors and collecting. | Treasure troves.
Classification: LCC NK5439.S34 B55 2017 | DDC 745.58/4—dc23 LC record available at https://lccn.loc.gov/2016059478

The Countryman Press
www.countrymanpress.com
A division of W. W. Norton & Company, Inc.
500 Fifth Avenue, New York, NY 10110
www.wwnorton.com

978-1-68268-116-9 (pbk.)

10 9 8 7 6 5 4 3 2 1